CHRISTMAS 2022

25 INSPIRING ADVENT THOUGHTS

SAMUEL PATRO

Contents

Contents

Foreword

Christmas, the most awaited occasion around the world as the year draws to a close, is today celebrated more as an excuse for merrymaking with the focus firmly on commerce. As we enter the festive season with the yuletide music ringing in our ears, the true meaning of Christmas is lost on most people.

And to think that the birth of Jesus Christ sent the message to the world that God had planned to come to the rescue of humanity. It said man was not without hope. It became the greatest event in the world calendar scripting the greatest love story ever told.

A.W.Tozer wrote: 'Man is lost but not abandoned. Had men not been lost, no Saviour would have been required. Had they been abandoned no Saviour would have come.'

'Christmas 2022' authored by an eminent writer, poet, and composer Mr. Samuel Patro points today's world in the direction of the manger. At a time when the world is torn apart by a multitude of tragedies including poverty, hunger, disease, pollution, hatred, dissension, exploitation, conflict and war, the birth of Jesus some 2000 years ago is the only hope available to mankind today.

My relationship and interaction with Mr. Patro, spanning more than half a century, has enabled me to share his deep longing for solutions to the overwhelming misery that surrounds us. The cry for an escape window from a world in flames, has troubled him continuously. And the solution is found in Jesus Christ, the crucified and risen saviour.

This book is an expression of his longing for a change in the world that is only possible through the transforming power of the gospel.

The thoughts expressed, one at a time, over a span of 25 days in the run-up to Christmas take us through the Biblical truth as the words of Jesus ring in our ears: 'I am the way, the truth and the life' (John 14:6). For the believer in Christ, Jesus is a brother, a friend, a healer and a teacher, the ultimate epitome of compassion, a word which has been rapidly losing its meaning in this world.

The love of God for fallen humanity has come alive in the dramatic birth and ministry of Jesus. He stands at the door of every person's heart today gently knocking for permission to come in.

Have you answered the call? A positive response alone can make the transformation of the human heart possible.

The question that needs an answer at this moment is: 'Did he get in?'

Paresh K. Das
Journalist

ppp

Preface

Christmas commemorates the birth of Jesus. Christmas also reminds us that the Creator entered His creation. God became man. It is a time of God sharing His great love for us.

"For God so loved the world that he gave his one and only Son, that whoever believes in him shall not perish but have eternal life" (John 3:16).

He is the Prince of Peace, the world's Saviour. He came to this world to mend our broken relationship with the Heavenly Father and to reconcile us to Him.

But how many of us truly understand the meaning of Christmas? The transformation He desires in us is only possible when we hand over the throne of our hearts to Him, the Prince of Peace, the Saviour. Have we allowed Him in? Let us consider it if we have not already.

"Christmas 2022" is a compilation of 25 Advent thoughts from the 1st to the 25th of December. I pray this book will heal many broken and wounded hearts and instil the living hope to enjoy the Love, Joy, and Peace of true Christmas.

Samuel Patro
Author

ϸϸϸ

Acknowledgements

Being an Octogenarian, I am ever grateful to Almighty God for His unfailing grace that has sustained me till date and kept my passion alive for writing. The medium of language of all my literary works over the last six decades is in Odia only.

Recently, for the first time in our family, my nephew Chiradeep Patra's book of poems was published in English by Notion Press. It was well appreciated by the readers. Since then, he only encouraged me to write a book in English. I have no hesitation to mention that "*Christmas 2022*" is a symbolic expression of his motivation and inspiration.

I am indebted to well-known journalist Mr. Paresh Das for his magnanimous gesture to write the Foreword of my book. In my literary journey, Mr. Das has been a real source of inspiration in many ways.

I am grateful to Mr. Ullas Pradhan, Founder of SMART-EDGE Spoken English, Personality Development and Abacus Academy whose helpful suggestions, wise counsel and editorial expertise have added to the beauty of this book.

Chiradeep has given his best for the total production of this book, i.e., its format, layout, cover design etc. He deserves my admiration and praise.

My dear wife Aruna has been my strong support all through my literary journey. A big thank you to Aruna. I also acknowledge the loving encouragement of my son Anurag and daughter-in-law Namrata.

Samuel Patro
Author

ONE
DID HE GET IN ?

Revelation 3:20 depicts a well-known picture of Jesus knocking at the door. The artist skillfully arranged the lights and shadows to form the outline of a heart. It indicates that Jesus is asking to enter into the heart. When a little girl saw this picture, she asked, *"Did He Get In?"*

In today's selfish, ambitious, materialistic and intolerant world impacted by the ruthless onslaught of the deadly coronavirus, we have developed a tendency to isolate ourselves.

When Jesus knocks at our hearts, He finds that people do not want to receive Him. His own people are either busy elsewhere and ignore Him or procrastinate answering. John writes, *"He came to His Own, And His Own didn't receive Him. But as many as received Him, to them He gave the right to become children of God, to those who believe in His name."*

This is advent. We are eagerly waiting for Christ's coming. Psalmist says, *"Lift up your heads you Gates! And be lifted up, you everlasting doors! And the King of Glory shall come in. Who is this King of Glory? The Lord of Hosts, He is the King of Glory."*

The coming days are exciting and a time of joyful anticipation. Christ is coming. Let us prepare our hearts to welcome Him and receive Him.

❦❦❦

TWO
PROMISED SAVIOUR

The Book of Isaiah is known as the miniature Bible. It contains sixty six chapters. The first thirty nine chapters deal with Judgment upon immoral men and the last twenty seven chapters declare a message of Hope.

Isaiah, the "St. Paul of the Old Testament" was a distinguished poet and prophet. His ministry commenced from 740 to 680 B.C. Isaiah is also called as "Shakespeare of the Prophet" and "Evangelical Prophet". Prophet Isaiah has the distinct honour of describing the birth, death and resurrection of the Promised Saviour Jesus Christ.

> "*For to us a child has been born, to us a son has been given; and the rule will be on his shoulder; and his name will be called Wonderful Counselor, Mighty God, Everlasting Father, Prince of Peace. (Isaiah 9:6)*"

In the above mentioned passage, Isaiah has vividly portrayed the character of Christ, the Saviour of mankind. He shall appear as a child. He is also a son. In Him, there is a perfect blending of both human and divine nature. He was unique in His conception, birth, preaching, miracles, suffering, death, resurrection and ascension because He was the manifestation of God.

Moreover, He was a Counselor. He expounded the law, instructed the people, pleaded for the guilty and appeared in the presence of God for men. He is the mighty God. He is the Prince of Peace. He rules by peace which leads to perfection and prosperity.

Thank God. What a wonderful Saviour we have! This is an illustrious prophecy of the incarnation of Christ.

ܒܒܒ

THREE
BETHLEHEM

Bethlehem is a household name synonymous with the birth of Jesus Christ. Prophet Micah's ministry ranged from about 735-710 BC and he highlighted Bethlehem, the birthplace of Jesus in his prophecy in the following words -

> *"But you, Bethlehem Ephrathah, Though you are little among the thousands of Judah, Yet out of you shall come forth to Me The One to be Ruler in Israel, Whose goings forth are from of old, From everlasting."*

Here is a small tribute to Bethlehem –

Bethlehem, "House of Bread"
Though small, yet beautiful
Endowed with Nature's bounty,
Green pastures, Blue sky add to your beauty.
After a tiring day,
In Nature's lap when you quietly lie,
The silent stars go by your night's sky.
But that night appeared
A bright shining star
That changed the course of mankind,
The angelic voice brought the good news

Of the birth of Christ Child.
Heaven's window was wide open,
Heavenly Father looked to this dark world
With loving concern.
A new way was open to Calvary
And the name of little town of Bethlehem
Was written in golden letters
In the world's history.

ԾԾԾ

FOUR
PREPARE THE WAY

God sent John the Baptist to prepare the way for Jesus. Several prophecies distinctly mention the mission of John the Baptist, the forerunner of the ministry of Jesus. Isaiah declares,

> *"A voice of one calling:*
> *"In the wilderness prepare*
> *the way for the Lord;*
> *make straight in the desert*
> *a highway for our God."*

John's message was direct and convincing. He preached repentance. He did not spare the feelings of the listeners but sincerely tried to help them in solving their spiritual problems. John preached the gospel when he pointed to Jesus and said, *"Behold the lamb of God that takes away the sin of the world."* Then he told the people to demonstrate their repentance by living true Christian lives.

Today, the voice of repentance is weak and hesitant. The message of repentance is seldom preached from the pulpit and if preached it is "shunned"! Sin is equated with common mistakes. John began his public preaching by saying, *"repent and believe the Gospel."* That must be also our message. Neither John nor Jesus was named "most popular preacher of the year." Their mission was not to please the people but to help them. John was humble and he believed in simple living.

Let's pray to God Almighty to enrich our lives with these qualities.

ᎠᎠᎠ

FIVE
TICKED OFF THE LIST

It is time again to send Christmas goodies and wishes. Last year's Christmas list is being compared. Arguments linger. *"They forgot last year, so we won't send them one this year."* But no Christmas message can say *"I have ticked you off my list of friends, you are still my friend."*

Fortunately, God has no such list. He extends His offer of His grace and mercy to all. He does not categorize people as worthy or unworthy because they belong to a particular race, or class or group, region, or gender.

God saw a world of rebels, all disobedient and wayward, all dressed in the dirty rags of their misdeeds. And yet He loved each one of them: even the very last one. He loved this ugly, wicked, and ungrateful world of people. God loved His enemies. God helped those who hurt and hated Him. There is nobody in the world that God does not love.

> *"Wide wide as the ocean*
> *High as the heaven above*
> *Deep deep as the deepest sea*
> *Is my Saviour's love."*

This is a beautiful rendition of God's impartial love.

Can I show love without prejudice to people who are "different?"

ﬠﬠﬠ

SIX

DIAGNOSIS AND CURE

The doctor examined the patient in the emergency room. With a grave look on his face, he told him "You have swallowed a deadly poison. You are critically ill. Unless you receive treatment at once, you will die."

This is the condition of those who try to find salvation through good works or "Karma". But this cannot save us. Our law of the land or good works convince us that we are hopelessly lost and helpless to do anything. The law offers no cure, no help, and no solution to escape the dire consequences of the spiritual poison of sin.

Spiritually, the cure for sin is the good news that Jesus was born in this world, took our sins on Himself and ultimately died on the cross for the remission of our sins. This is the Christmas message – when the world was dying in sin, God provided the remedy – His only Son.

Do I sometimes make the mistake of thinking that God will save me because "I try to do the best I can?"

ᖚᖚᖚ

SEVEN
WHAT A BIRTHDAY PARTY

Imagine a birthday party. Refreshments and cakes were served. But some selfish children ate all the ice cream without giving it to the birthday boy. Everyone congratulated and wished him well, but the birthday boy was ignored and devoid of his snacks.

Are we about to celebrate Jesus' birthday party like that? People give Christmas gifts to themselves, their families and their relatives. What does Jesus get? They entertain their friends and enjoy themselves. Where does Jesus fit in their plans?

Selfishness often characterizes the observance of the most unselfish act of God – the giving of His Son. Everything God did at Christmas was unselfish. Jesus was not born in a Hi-tech hospital. He was born in a stable. Later, He did not have a place to lay His head. He rode a borrowed donkey on Palm Sunday. He rented the room where He instituted the Lord's Supper. He was buried in a borrowed grave. He lived for others. He died for others. He came to serve others.

My Christmas celebrations will be more fulfilling if I prioritize Jesus and put myself last. The best definition of JOY is Jesus, Others, and You.

ᏘᏘᏘ

EIGHT
ANARCHY

Consider the case where the traffic signal at a busy intersection fails to function. Traffic is backed up. Soon cars are boxed in and nobody can move. A policeman begins directing the traffic. Soon the cars move again. When every motorist does what he feels, it does not work. When they follow instructions, everybody moves – life is smooth.

God gave the world laws, principles and commandments to enable people to live together in good order and harmony. To defy these universal laws is to invite chaos, disorder and punishment.

Quite a number of people today believe that an individual can lead a life as he pleases. It means they disregard God's laws. Then human life becomes cheap, disorderly and chaotic. History tells us that civilizations crumbled, nations were destroyed, and races perished because people defied God's laws.

Our God is a God of discipline and orderliness. Even the birth of Jesus was well planned and well timed. The ministry of Jesus in this world was also carried on in a disciplined manner.

Lord, help me to obey your laws to lead an orderly life.

NINE
ZECHARIAH

An angel appeared to the aged priest, Zechariah, as he was officiating at the altar and told him that his wife Elizabeth would bear a child. Zechariah could not believe this because both he and his wife were advanced in age, and it was contrary to their nature to have a child at their age. Therefore, he asked for a sign to prove the truth of the angel's message. Then he became dumb.

Zechariah forgot how God had blessed Sarah with a child in her old age and how God had heard Hannah's prayer and had given her a son. He could not believe because he thought if a human being can not do it, neither can God. This is often our problem. We judge God's ability by our own limitations. When something seems impossible to us, or in violation of all past experience, we conclude it must also be impossible for God.

God is always doing miraculous things. Listen to the angel! *"With God, nothing will be impossible."*

Zechariah received his sign. He was unable to speak until the child was born.

Do I sometimes make God too small in my life by thinking that if I cannot do it, God can't either? Forgive me God for my narrow and immature thinking.

ﬖﬖﬖ

TEN
HISTORY REPEATS

The world situation during the time of the birth of Jesus was the same as it is today. There were wars, crime, pollution, communal violence, hatred, abuse, exploitation, etc.

The world was evil and furious. When Herod heard the news about the birth of Jesus, he was furious. He ordered that all the male children in Bethlehem, two years and under should be murdered. The two men crucified with Jesus were criminals. Jesus referred to those whose blood Pilate had mingled with their sacrifices.

One News Paper columnist writes *"We live in an age of Rage."* Even today, the world situation hasn't changed. There's exploitation, war, communal violence, hatred and mass revolution. The ongoing war between Russia and Ukraine has not yet subsided. We are living in a dangerous time. We still look for some magic solution to make the world better.

Christ's coming did not automatically change the world into a paradise. But anyone who accepts Christ will be a "new creature," who seeks to do God's will. God gives us the power to love and live in harmony. When God directs a person's life, then that person becomes an effective tool to influence others.

Lord, help me to exert my influence to improve my surroundings.

ৡৡৡ

ELEVEN

AUGUSTUS

The Roman Emperor ordered for a census for the purpose of taxation. Augustus was not interested in God, or the Messiah or the Old Testament prophets, but God used Him for His purposes.

Each person was required to go to his ancestral town. Since Mary and Joseph were descendants of David, they went from Nazareth to Bethlehem.

Mary was pregnant and was soon to give birth, but they had to make this journey to obey the orders of the Emperor. Because of his decree, Jesus was born in Bethlehem and not in Nazareth.

God is always involved in the activities of the nations. His finger moves the course of the world so that His plans are carried out. God has not lost the control of world situation. As God used the Roman Emperor to fulfill His purposes, He still directs the affairs of the world today also. He assures us with these words, "Be still and know that I am God".

Today, things look bad in the world. But we are confident that God directs our lives, and the affairs of the world because "the Lord of hosts is with us."

Let us pray diligently for our country and the world.

ᐅᐅᐅ

TWELVE
MARY

Christmas reminds us of the wonderful song of Boney M –

> **"Long time ago in Bethlehem**
> **So the Holy Bible say, Mary's boy child Jesus Christ**
> **Was born on Christmas day."**

This song portrays Mary as the central character in the story of the birth of Christ.

Mary was a common name in Palestine during the first century. But in spite of her ordinary name, Mary the mother of Jesus was an extraordinary woman. She hailed from a peasant family. Mary humbly accepted God's message and expressed her strong belief in God's message. "But when the time had fully come, God sent His Son born of a woman" (Gal 4:4).

Mary is best known for

- Her obedience to God's message through the angel Gabriel.
- Becoming the earthly mother of Jesus Christ though she was a virgin.
- Her consistent presence with Jesus throughout his life. (Luke 1:46-55)

Mary's song is known as "Magnificat". Magnificat in Latin means "Glorifies" or "Magnifies". It can be compared with the song of Hannah (1 Samuel 2:1-10).

In these songs, these two women glorify the Lord for favouring them in their humble state for His mercy and mighty deeds and for caring for the downtrodden. Mary appears at different points during her son's life, ministry trial and crucifixion.

ᖰᖰᖰ

THIRTEEN

JOSEPH

Joseph was an honourable person, a man of integrity and high moral standard. He was shocked to hear that Mary was pregnant. He was mentally disturbed because they did not live together as man and wife.

What was he to do? Soon her disgrace would become evident. Should Joseph let the law take its course? He decided that he would dissolve the relationship between them and put Mary away quietly.

But what looked like disgrace and dishonour to Joseph was part of God's redemptive plan for the whole of mankind. God's angel assured him that Mary had not been unfaithful and that he should accept her as his wife.

Max Lucado beautifully explains Joseph's action plan in the following words:

> "*Obey, that's what he did. He obeyed. He obeyed when the angel called. He obeyed when Mary explained. He obeyed when God sent. He was obedient to God. He was obedient when the sky was bright. He was obedient when the sky was dark.*"

Mary and Joseph demonstrated obedience and devotion to God's commands. When the child was circumcised on the Eighth day, Mary and Joseph gave him the name Jesus in obedience to Gabriel's instructions (Luke 2:21).

"TRUST AND OBEY"

✹✹✹

FOURTEEN

INNKEEPER

Scores of people were converging on Bethlehem to comply with the census order of Emperor Augustus. Soon all the rooms in the inn were filled. More people kept coming. What would the Inn Keeper do? Today, he would display the "No Vacancy" sign.

Our natural tendency is to condemn the innkeeper as unkind and cruel because he turned Joseph and Mary away in the hour of their need. Where should the innkeeper have put Mary and Joseph?

Let us consider the guests. Perhaps they were selfish because they did not give their room to Mary and Joseph. Neither the innkeeper nor the guests could realize that this young woman would that night give birth to the son of God. Mary and Joseph were just another couple and Mary was just another expectant mother to them.

The innkeeper did not want to disturb the paying guests. Therefore, he put Joseph and Mary in the stable. Those who had rooms did not want to give up their comfort for the sake of an unknown couple. The lack of concern for the people in need is the same today as it was on the first Christmas night. When we call it "non-involvement", it is still plain selfishness.

Lord, forgive my selfishness. Make me more sensitive to understand the need of others.

ᐅᐅᐅ

FIFTEEN
WHAT'S IN A NAME ?

A man named Joy may be an angry person and a man named Sundar may be an unappealing person. A name usually does not always describe an individual.

But the name given to Mary's son describes Him perfectly. The angel proclaimed *"You shall call His name JESUS, for He will save His people from their sins."* Jesus means one who saves, delivers and helps others.

The other name applied to Jesus is IMMANUEL, which means, "God with us." It is hard to think of the little boy born to Mary as being Immanuel, God with us. We celebrate Christmas, not because a child was born in a stable and wrapped in cloths, but because that child was Immanuel - God with us in human form, in our own flesh and blood.

There are two basic truths of the Christian faith:

- This little child who came into the world is Immanuel – the Son of God.
- This Son of God is Jesus – Our Saviour.

On these two great truths rest our faith, hope, comfort, assurance and salvation.

The birth of Jesus was a great divider of history, i.e., B.C. and A.D. Jesus, help me to sort out the essence of Christmas.

ᗉᗉᗉ

SIXTEEN

HOME FOR CHRISTMAS

Christmas is a time for home coming. It is a sad Christmas for those who can't get home due to distance, employment or personal disadvantages. Some have no home to which they can go. Others are not welcome at their homes.

People rush to go home. What attracts them? At home there is love, warmth, friendliness and the sense of belonging. At home, one finds a loving and caring family atmosphere.

Home should also be the place of God's presence. The risen Christ walked along the road with the two disciples. They asked him to abide with them. So, He went to stay with them. Happy is the home where Jesus goes in to stay with the family. He should not be a guest because guest is not a member of the family. *"Behold, I stand at the door and knock, if any one hears my voice and opens the door, I will come into him and eat with him and he with me"* (Revelation 3:20). A home where people are for each other is wonderful. Unfortunately, many homes are destroyed today because of broken families. We can be happy under any circumstance if Jesus comes into our life.

What is Jesus to me? A casual visitor? A frequent Guest? A partner in my life?

ᘐᘐᘐ

SEVENTEEN
CHRISTMAS SPIRIT

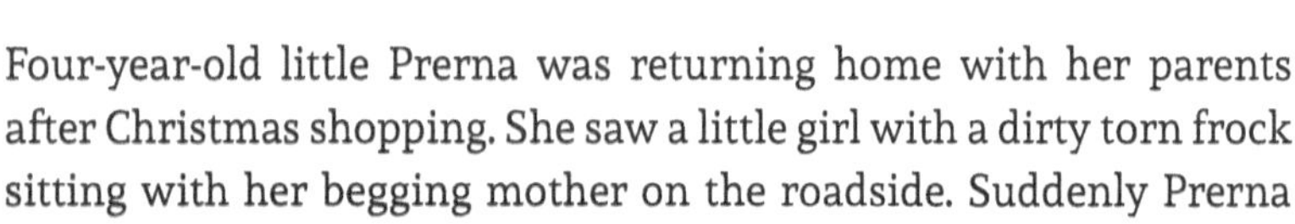

Four-year-old little Prerna was returning home with her parents after Christmas shopping. She saw a little girl with a dirty torn frock sitting with her begging mother on the roadside. Suddenly Prerna stopped and looked at the girl. Then she said, *"Dad, can we buy a frock for this little child?"* It was a stirring question.

During Christmas, we visit the poor and the sick. We sing for them and give them gifts. But what do we do for them in other times?

We forget the needy so easily because we can't put ourselves into their shoes. We can't experience the pain of a sightless or deaf person. What is our concern for the sick, the aged, the differently abled and the forsaken in our society? Our expression of loving concern during Christmas is only a seasonal momentary emotion.

Think for a moment how much of Jesus' ministry was devoted to the sick, the needy and the despised. It was possible because of His love and compassion. Compassion is God's heart. Mother Teresa once said, *"Love till it hurts."*

Why do I so easily slip back to selfish indifference towards the needy as soon as Christmas is over?

Let us imbibe in us the perennial Christmas spirit.

ppp

EIGHTEEN
DO NOT BE AFRAID

Fear is an innate human instinct. It has debilitated the world's most powerful as well as richest individuals and nations. But the angelic message, "Do not be afraid", has been repeated on three different occasions in connection with the Christmas story in the gospel according to Luke.

First, the angel appeared to Zachariah in the temple and proclaimed this message when he announced the birth of John the Baptist. Then the angel proclaimed the same message to Mary and finally, the angel appeared to the Shepherds and said, *"Do not be afraid, for behold I bring you good tidings of great joy."*

What a message at a time like this when we lived behind locked doors during Covid-19 in great fear and disaster! The fear of death crippled the whole universe.

We live in dangerous times. Every day, the newspaper carries stories of violence, hatred, murder, exploitation, killing and inhuman atrocities. We face a fearful and critical situation because of terrorism, war and natural disasters caused by climate change.

Christ came to this world to make peace between God and man. The Christmas message is Good News, designed to bring great joy to all who need it. God came at Christmas time in all His love and mercy. He did not come to destroy, but to deliver.

God assures us today also with the words – *Do not be afraid, I am your friend. I am coming to your rescue. Look up! Cheer up! Unto you is born a Saviour.*

Lord, remove my fear. Strengthen my faith in you.

ᔭᔭᔭ

NINETEEN
WISE MEN

The Bible tells us that wise men from the East, led by a star, came to Jerusalem to inquire where the King of Jews had been born. They were directed to Bethlehem and found the child. They worshipped Him, offered Him their gifts and returned home.

Many stories have been invented to exaggerate this simple account. The Bible does not describe them as Kings, or Soothsayers. The Bible attaches no symbolic meaning to the gifts they presented to Christ.

One thing does stand out – God very definitely guided these wise men. They were acquainted with the prophecies of the Messiah. God led them by a miraculous star, which finally stood over the stable where baby Jesus was born. God then directed them to return home another way. Herod's sinister plan was spoiled.

God led shepherds from Bethlehem and wise men from a distant land to Saviour. In this time of religious confusion, we need a star to lead us directly to Jesus. We have one – the Word. The Word became flesh and dwelt with us. (John 1:14). Christ said, "*I am the way, the truth and life.*" If we follow God's directions, we will find the Saviour.

Lord, let your word guide me directly to my Saviour.

♥♥♥

TWENTY
SILENT NIGHT

"Silent Night, Holy Night", the most acclaimed beloved Christmas Carol has a beautiful story.

Joseph Mohr, the hymn writer was a young pastor of a village Church at Obermdorf in Austria. The year was 1818. Christmas was drawing near. The young Pastor was preparing his Christmas sermon at night. There was a gentle knock at the door. Mohr opened the door. There appeared a member of his Parish from a distant Alpine village. The visitor pleaded "Sir, my wife has delivered a son. She has sent me with a request to take you home to bless the child. Kindly come with me."

Young Pastor paused for a moment and decided to accompany the visitor. It was heavily snowing. They crossed the jungle and reached the village home. A candle was lit in the tiny little room. The newborn babe slept peacefully on his mother's lap. The Pastor offered the prayer and left. But he could not forget the beautiful scene of that silent night. On his return, he composed this beautiful song.

The next day he met his friend Franz Grubber who was a Pianist and Music Composer. Mr. & Mrs. Grubber highly praised this beautiful song and composed the music. They both presented this Carol in the Church on Christmas Day. Within a short span of time, this song was widely appreciated as alltime favourite Christmas Carol and subsequently, it has been translated into three hundred languages around the world.

Can we impact our society with our silent but effective actions in today's busy world?

ᗧᗧᗧ

TWENTY-ONE
SACRIFICIAL LOVE

Middle-aged Akash has given up everything to care for his wife Varsha. They knew that life has slowly deteriorated with Varsha's early detection of Cancer. Akash has rearranged his schedule to care for her more effectively. He cooks, cleans, bathes, and administers medicine and makes sure that Varsha can get to and from the bathroom with her weak body. He cherishes her in sickness, health, disappointment, and frailty. Driven by great love he gives his selfless service to her.

This selfless sacrificial service is only possible when we are today in love with Jesus. He takes control of our life. Jesus Christ is the greatest loving gift of God the father to this world. *"For God so loved the world that he gave His only begotten son..."* (John 3:16). When we truly love Jesus, our hearts become devoted to Him.

Corrie Ten Boom endured brutal treatment in World War II Concentration Camp. Although her father and sister died while imprisoned by Nazis, Corrie's love lived on, sustained by God whose love never ends. She has expressed her explicit love and commitment to God in those powerful words: *"Do you know what hurts so very much? It's love. Love is the strongest force in the world and when it is blocked, that means pain."*

In the midst of carnage and calamity, Jeremiah was able to claim *"The faithful love of the Lord never ends! His mercies never cease."* (Lamentation 3:22).

Let us not lose heart and accept the Christmas challenge to serve Him unconditionally.

❦❦❦

TWENTY-TWO
GOD WITH US

"Christ with me, Christ before me, Christ behind me,
Christ within me, Christ beneath me, Christ above me,
Christ at my right, Christ at my left..."

The words of this hymn, written by the fifth-century Christian writer St. Patrick became vibrant when we read Mathew's account of Jesus' birth. They remind us that we are never alone.

Mathew's account quotes Isaiah's prophecy of a child who would be called Immanuel, meaning *"God with us"* (Isaiah 7:14). Mathew points to the ultimate fulfilment of that prophecy – Jesus, the one born by the power of the Holy Spirit to be God with us. This truth is so central that Mathew begins and ends his gospel with it. The concluding remarks of Jesus to His disciples were *"And surely I am with you always, to the very end of the age"* (Matt. 28:20).

St. Patrick's hymn assures us that Christ lives always with His believers through His Spirit. When we are in trouble, when we are afraid or disappointed, we can hold fast to His promises that He will never leave us. During our celebrations and joyous moments, we thank Him for His everlasting grace and mercy in our lives.

Jesus, Immanuel – God with us. God's love became incarnate at Bethlehem.

TWENTY-THREE
AMAZING GRACE

We come now to a profound verse which has been central to our thinking this Christmas.

> *"The word became flesh and dwelt among us and we beheld His glory, the glory of the only begotten of the Father, full of grace and truth (John 1:14)."*

Selwin Hughes, the founder of CWR explains the concept of grace in the most powerful manner as mentioned below: -

> *"The first element of the Christian faith is grace - an act of outgoing, forgiving love. The first characteristic of God is love, and grace is love reaching down to a lost humanity in Jesus Christ. It is the word of love that became flesh. Grace is simply unmerited favour. Grace is love favouring us when we are not favourable, loving us when we are not lovable, accepting us when we are not acceptable, redeeming us when we are not redeemable."*

According to Theologian John Wallace,

> *"Although the favourite word of angels might be love, the favourite word of the sinner is grace. Love reaches out on the*

same level, but grace always bends to pick us up. Grace is love applied, the word of love became flesh."

Father God, how grateful I am for your grace. Help me to extend your grace through me to others.

ᐁᐁᐁ

TWENTY-FOUR
CHRISTMAS EVE

It was Christmas Eve 1944. A man known as "Old Brinker" lay dying in Muntak Prison, Sumatra. He was waiting for the makeshift Christmas Service led by fellow prisoners. He asked his fellow prisoner when does the music start?" "*Soon*" replied his friend. "*Good*", replied the dying man. "*Then I will be able to compare them with the angels.*" Brinker died after the choir of eleven fragile and weak bodied prisoners sang his request, "Silent Night." Although Brinker moved away from his faith in God for a long time, in his dying days he confessed his sins and found peace in Him.

In his book "Joyful and Triumphant" the famous well known theologian and Christian thinker Late Dr. M. M. Thomas has described that he lost his dear wife Annama Thomas in Vellore Hospital on December 24th at midnight when this Christmas song **"O, come all ye faithful, Joyful and Triumphant"** was being played in the hospital campus. Mrs. Thomas was a committed Christian and was suffering from cancer.

What a great paradox of human life!

Perhaps death has been a welcome Christmas visitor to both old Brinker and Mrs. Thomas.

May God help us to understand the mystery of joy in the midst of pain.

ﬔﬔﬔ

TWENTY-FIVE

JOY

Joy is a powerful theme of Christmas.

We know the story of the boy who stood looking at the picture of his deceased father. Then turning with ecstatic joy to his mother he said wistfully, "I wish father would step out of the picture and hold me in his arms." That young boy expressed the kind of deep longings of the human heart as we stand looking at the picture frame of the universe and want our Father to step out of the picture and meet us as a person.

The good news of great joy is that the father has stepped out of the picture. This is the meaning of Christmas. Jesus is Immanuel – God with us. The wonder of Christmas is that God, who dwelt among us, now can dwell with in us. The good news of joy is that Christ's coming has brought forgiveness, life, hope and salvation for all of us. The gift is ours. We can sing, shout and rejoice today because God so loved the world that He gave His only begotten son for us. This is another reason for joy.

The challenge of Christmas 22' is – Do I have the inner joy of experiencing the living presence of Christ?

Wish you a Blessed and Joyous Christmas.